mel bay prese

OLD-TIME GOSPEL
BANJO SOLOS

Thirty-One all-time gospel favorites
arranged in three-finger style

by Jack Hatfield

CD CONTENTS

1. Introduction
2. Tuning the Banjo

UP-TEMPO, WITH ACCOMPANIMENT

3. A Beautiful Life
4. Abide With Me
5. Amazing Grace
6. Angel Band
7. Are You Washed in the Blood?
8. Crying Holy Unto the Lord
9. Drifting Too Far From the Shore
10. Farther Along
11. The Great Speckled Bird
12. He Leadeth Me!
13. Holy, Holy, Holy!
14. I Am A Pilgrim
15. In The Garden
16. In The Sweet By and By
17. Just A Closer Walk With Thee
18. Just Over in The Glory Land
19. Keep On The Sunny Side Of Life
20. Life's Railway to Heaven
21. The Lily of the Valley

22. The Old Gospel Ship
23. The Old Rugged Cross
24. Old-Time Religion
25. Precious Memories
26. Rock Of Ages
27. Shall We Gather at the River
28. Sweet Hour of Prayer
29. The Unclouded Day
30. What a Friend We Have in Jesus
31. When the Roll is Called Up Yonder
32. Where the Soul of Man Never Dies
33. Will The Circle Be Unbroken?

LEARNING SPEED, BANJO ONLY

34. Crying Holy Unto The Lord
35. In The Sweet By And By
36. Just Over In The Glory Land
37. Keep On The Sunny Side Of Life
38. Old-Time Religion
39. The Unclouded Day
40. When The Roll Is Called Up Yonder
41. Where The Soul Of Man Never Dies
42. Will The Circle Be Unbroken?

1 2 3 4 5 6 7 8 9 0

Visit us on the Web at www.melbay.com — E-mail us at email@melbay.com

Table Of Contents

A Note On Tunings

The G and C tunings are used throughout this book. The specific tuning for each song is noted on its title page above the first measure.

Example: G tuning = gDGBD

C tuning = gCGBD

Introduction

This book contains thirty-one of the most loved old-time gospel songs, complete with musical notation, banjo tablature, chords, and lyrics. There is something here for banjoists of all ability levels. Each song is presented first as a beginner-intermediate arrangement, played in the first position, in Scruggs style. Most songs are then presented in a more challenging up-the-neck arrangement. All arrangements are strictly melody - oriented. There are no "hot licks" or flashy fill-in licks to detract from the melody of these classic hymns. As such, this is a study in how to interpret vocal songs in Scruggs style so that the melody is preserved.

A feature of all my banjo books is boldface melody notes. If you emphasize the boldface notes, the melody will become more obvious, even at learning speed. If you are unfamiliar with the melody and are unable to read musical notation, you may play through the arrangement, sounding only the boldface notes. You will then be able to hear the melody as sung, and will be able to learn the banjo arrangement much more quickly. This procedure is also helpful in learning to sing the song correctly.

It is recommended that you listen intently to the recording that accompanies this book before learning the songs. You will reduce your learning time considerably if you already have the arrangement "in your head" before learning the tab. You will also hear emphasis and tonal variation that only listening can fully demonstrate. Listening before working on the tablature will also improve your learning "by ear" skills. Once you do start working from the tablature, you can use your remote control to cue up a particular song or to play a difficult passage over and over, without having to get up from your seat.

Whether you plan to play these arrangements in church, jam sessions, or simply to entertain yourself at home, I sincerely hope you enjoy and learn from them. Playing the five-string banjo is a wonderful way to make a joyful noise unto the Lord!

Jack Hatfield

Dedication

I would like to dedicate this book to Lois Hatfield, who, in her infinite mother's wisdom, forced me to attend Magnolia Avenue United Methodist Church in Knoxville, Tennessee. The clergy, youth directors, and members there took on the difficult and unenviable task of teaching me how to live a good life. The church survived...

Cover photo: Middle Creek United Methodist Church in Sevierville, Tennessee. Photos by Bill Armstrong

Jack Hatfield

ABOUT THE AUTHOR

Jack Hatfield has been a professional instructor of banjo and a *Banjo Newsletter* columnist for almost twenty-five years at the time of this printing. He has taught thousands to play the banjo via his instruction book series entitled *Bluegrass Banjo Method*. His *Scruggs Corner* columns analyzed the work of Earl Scruggs, the "father of bluegrass banjo". These transcriptions remain today the most complete and accurate body of Earl's recordings ever published. Jack then wrote the *Beginner's Corner* column in which he tutored novice banjoists. He is currently writing a column called *Concepts and Systems*, which explains the structure of music as applied to the five-string banjo and reveals procedures and systems of learning. Jack has also published a unique theory book for all musicians called *How to Play by Ear–A Guide to Chords and Progressions for Musicians, Songwriters, and Composers*. He has three other Mel Bay publications to his credit, *You Can Teach Yourself Banjo by Ear*, *You Can Teach Yourself Mandolin by Ear*, and *Rounder Old-Time Music for Banjo*.

Jack is band leader and banjoist for the *True Blue* bluegrass band, which works conventions and tourist attractions such as *Dollywood* theme park and the *Dixie Stampede* in his home town of Pigeon Forge, Tennessee. He has been a finalist in the *Tennessee State Banjo Championship*, the *Kentucky State Banjo Championship*, and the *National Banjo Championship* held in Winfield, Kansas. As director of *Banjo Newsletter Workshops*, he travels across the U.S.A., teaching and promoting banjo workshops featuring today's top recording artists and other *Banjo Newsletter* columnists.

HOW TO READ TABLATURE

Tablature is a method of writing music for stringed instruments that shows what notes to play graphically instead of by standard musical notation. Here is how it works:

Banjo tablature has five lines. Each line represents one of the banjo strings. The first (top) line represents the first (bottom) string of the banjo. The second line represents the second (from the bottom) string, and so on.

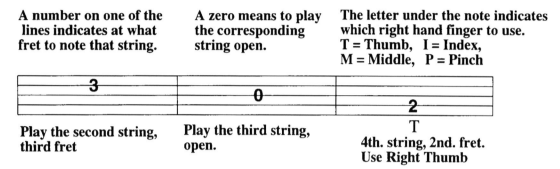

A number on one of the lines indicates at what fret to note that string.	A zero means to play the corresponding string open.	The letter under the note indicates which right hand finger to use. T = Thumb, I = Index, M = Middle, P = Pinch
Play the second string, third fret	Play the third string, open.	4th. string, 2nd. fret. Use Right Thumb

In problem areas, the suggested Left hand fingering will be shown by a lower case letter above the note.

A *beat* is a unit of time. All beats are equidistant in time unless noted by the composer. Beats are grouped into equal blocks called *measures* or *bars*. These are sectioned off by the use of vertical *measure lines* or *bar lines*, which make it easier to count time and keep your place. The *time signature*, which appears at the beginning of the tune in standard musical notation, can alter the number of beats per measure or the time allowed to the various note types. Almost all banjo tablature is written in 4/4 time, meaning there are four beats in each measure and a quarter note receives one beat. The time signature is usually not shown in banjo tablature unless the piece is in 3/4 time, in which there are three beats in each measure and a quarter note receives one beat.

Duration is indicated by the use of *stems*, *beams*, and *flags*. A *stem* is a vertical line attached to a note. A *beam* is a heavy horizontal line connecting two or more notes. A *flag* is a pennant-shaped mark attached to a stem. A note that stands alone with a stem is a *quarter note*. It lasts one full beat. A note that either has a single flag and stands alone or is attached to another note or notes by a single beam is an *eighth note*. It lasts one-half a beat. A note that either has two flags and stands alone or is attached to other notes by two beams is a *sixteenth note*. It lasts one fourth of a beat.

A large "squiggle" mark is a *quarter rest*. It denotes one beat of silence. A heavy dash attached to the third line is a *half rest*. It denotes two beats of silence. A *tie* is a curved line that connects two notes. It signifies that the first note is to be played and held the duration of both notes added together. For example, two quarter notes joined by a tie signify a single note that lasts two beats. The *chords* will be shown in bold type above the tablature. This is primarily for the rhythm players, but can give the lead player valuable hints about left hand fingering. *Melody notes* will be in boldface type. *Fill notes* will be in regular type. The Melody notes are to be played more loudly than the Fill notes. *Hammer-ons*, *pull-offs* and *slides* will be shown by a dash between two notes and the letter H, P or S underneath. A sample tablature appears below with features labeled.

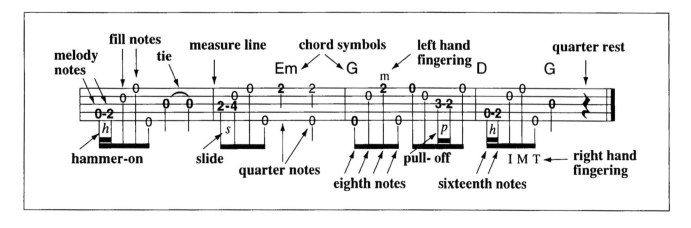

A Beautiful Life

William M. Golden

William M. Golden

Refrain:

Second Solo - Intermediate/Advanced Level

Verse:

Refrain:

A Beautiful Life

1) Each day I'll do a golden deed;
By helping those who are in need.
My life on Earth is but a span;
And so I'll do the best I can.

Refrain:
Bass: Life's evening sun is sinking low;
A few more days and I must go.
Lead: To meet the deeds that I have done;
Where there will be no setting sun.

2) To be a child of God each day;
My light must shine along the way.
I'll sing His praise while ages roll;
And strive to help some troubled soul.

Refrain

3) The only life that will endure;
Is one that's kind and good and pure.
And so for God I'll take my stand;
Each day I'll lend a helping hand.

Refrain

4) I'll help someone in time of need;
And journey on with rapid speed.
I'll help the sick, the poor and weak;
And words of kindness to them speak.

Refrain

5) While going down life's weary road;
I'll try to lift some traveler's load.
I'll try to turn the night to day;
Make flowers bloom along the way.

Refrain

Abide with Me

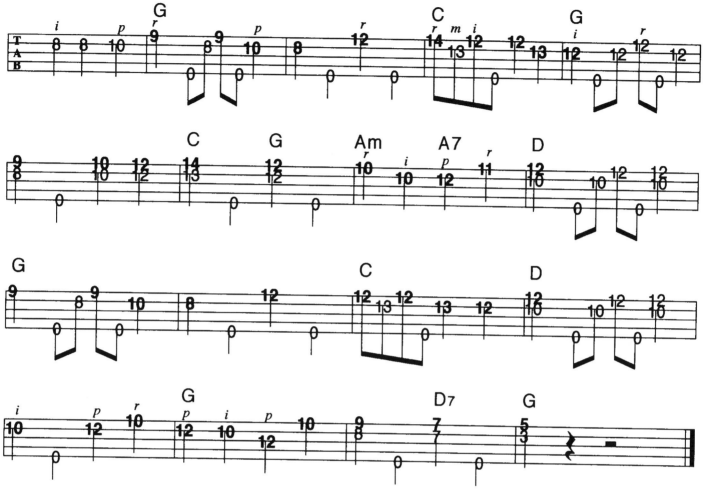

1) Abide with me; fast falls the eventide;
The darkness deepens; Lord, with me abide;
When other helpers fail, and comforts flee,
Help of the helpless, Oh, abide with me!

2) Swift to its close ebbs out life's little day;
Earth's joys grow dim, it's glories pass away,
Change and decay in all around I see;
Oh, thou who changes not abide with me!

3) I need thy presence every passing hour;
What but thy grace can foil the tempter's pow'r?
Who like thyself can guide and stay can be?
Thro' cloud and sunshine, abide with me!

4) Hold thou thy cross before my closing eyes;
Shine thro' the gloom and point me towards the skies.
Heav'n's morning breaks and earth's vain shadows flee;
In life, in death, O Lord, abide with me!

Second Solo - Intermediate Level

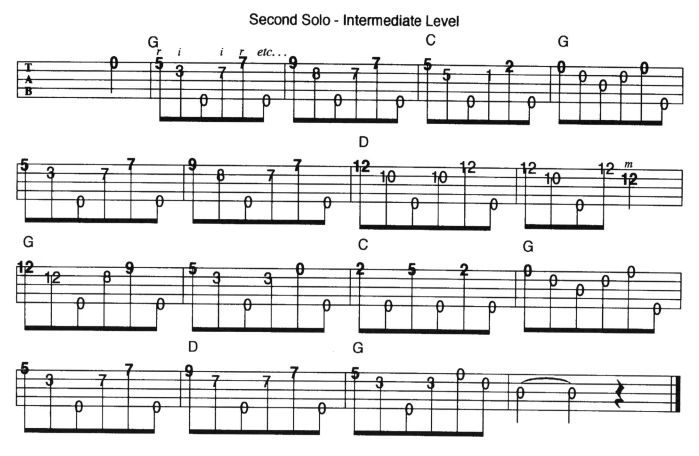

Third Solo -This is a chord melody. It has the same left hand
part as the Fourth Solo which follows.

( ) = Alternate chords, not played by rhythm instruments

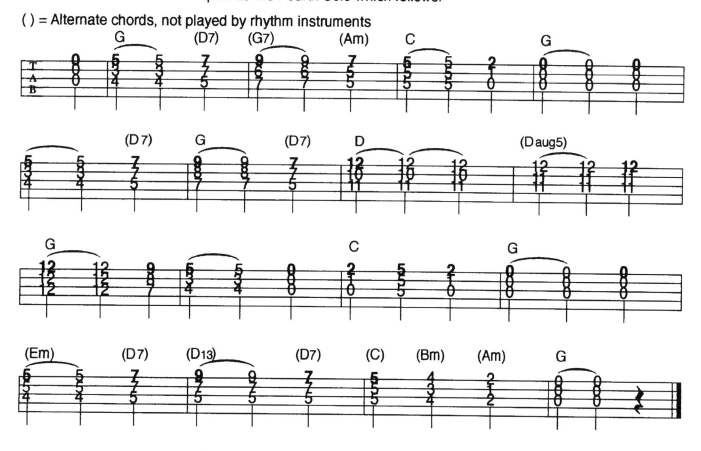

Fourth Solo - Advanced Level

( ) = Alternate chords

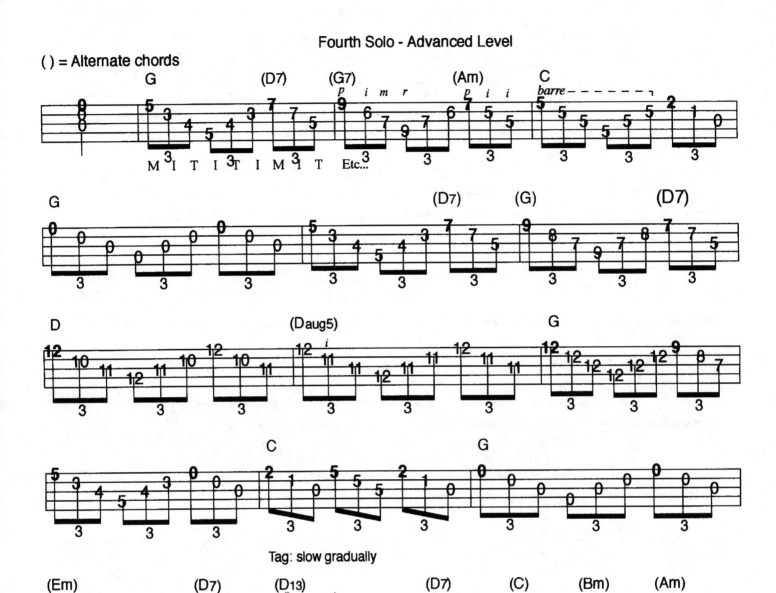

Tag: slow gradually

14

Amazing Grace

1) Amazing grace, how sweet the sound
That saved a wretch like me!
I once was lost but now am found,
Was blind but now I see.

2) 'Twas grace that taught my heart to fear,
And grace my fears relieved;
How precious did that grace appear,
The hour I first believed!

3) Through many dangers, toils and snares
I have already come;
'Tis grace has brought me safe thus far,
And grace will lead me home.

4) The Lord has promised good to me,
His word my hope secures;
He will my shield and portion be,
As long as life endures.

5) When we've been there ten thousand years,
Bright shining as the sun;
We've no less days to sing his praise,
Than when we first begun!

Angel Band

G Tuning:
DBGDg

Ability Level:
Beginner/Intermediate

Jefferson Hascall

William Batchelder Bradbury

Refrain:

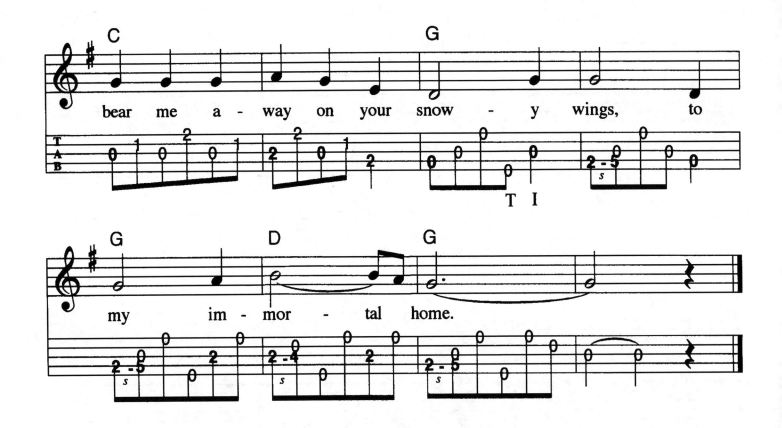

bear me a-way on your snow—y wings, to

my im - mor - tal home.

Angel Band

1) My latest sun is sinking fast,
My race is nearly run.
My strongest trials now are past,
My triumph has begun!

Refrain: Oh, come, angel band,
Come, and around me stand.
Oh, bear me away on your snowy wings,
To my immortal home.
Oh, bear me away on your snowy wings,
To my immortal home.

2) I've almost gained my heavenly home
My spirit loudly sings.
The holy ones behold they come!
I hear the voice of wings!
(Refrain)

3) Oh bear my longing heart to Him
Who bled and died for me.
Whose blood now cleanses from all sin
And gives me victory.
(Refrain)

Are You Washed In The Blood?

G Tuning:
DBGDg

Ability Level:
Beginner/Intermediate

Rev. E.A. Hoffman

Rev. E.A. Hoffman

Verse:

Refrain:

Are You Washed In The Blood?

1) Have you been to Jesus for the cleansing power?
Are you washed in the blood of the Lamb?
Are you fully trusting in His grace this hour?
Are you washed in the blood of the Lamb?

REFRAIN: Are you washed? (are you washed?) In the blood (in the blood)
In the soul-cleansing blood of the Lamb?
Are your garments spotless, are they white as snow?
Are you washed in the blood of the Lamb?

2) Are you walking daily by the Savior's side?
Are you washed in the blood of the Lamb?
Do you rest each moment in the Crucified?
Are you washed in the blood of the Lamb?

(REFRAIN)

3) When the Bridegroom cometh will your robes be white?
Are you washed in the blood of the Lamb?
Will your soul be ready for the mansion bright?
Are you washed in the blood of the Lamb?

(REFRAIN)

4) Lay aside the garments that are stained with sin;
And be washed in the blood of the Lamb.
There's a fountain flowing for the soul unclean;
Oh, be washed in the blood of the Lamb.

(REFRAIN)

Crying Holy Unto The Lord

Refrain:

1) Lord, I ain't no stranger now,
Lord, I ain't no stranger now.
I've been introduced to the Father and Son
Lord, I ain't no stranger now.

Refrain

2) Sinners run and hide your face,
Sinners run and hide your face.
Sinners run to the rock and hide your face,
Lord cried out "No hiding place".

Refrain

Drifting Too Far From The Shore

Charles E. Moody

Charles E. Moody

Refrain:

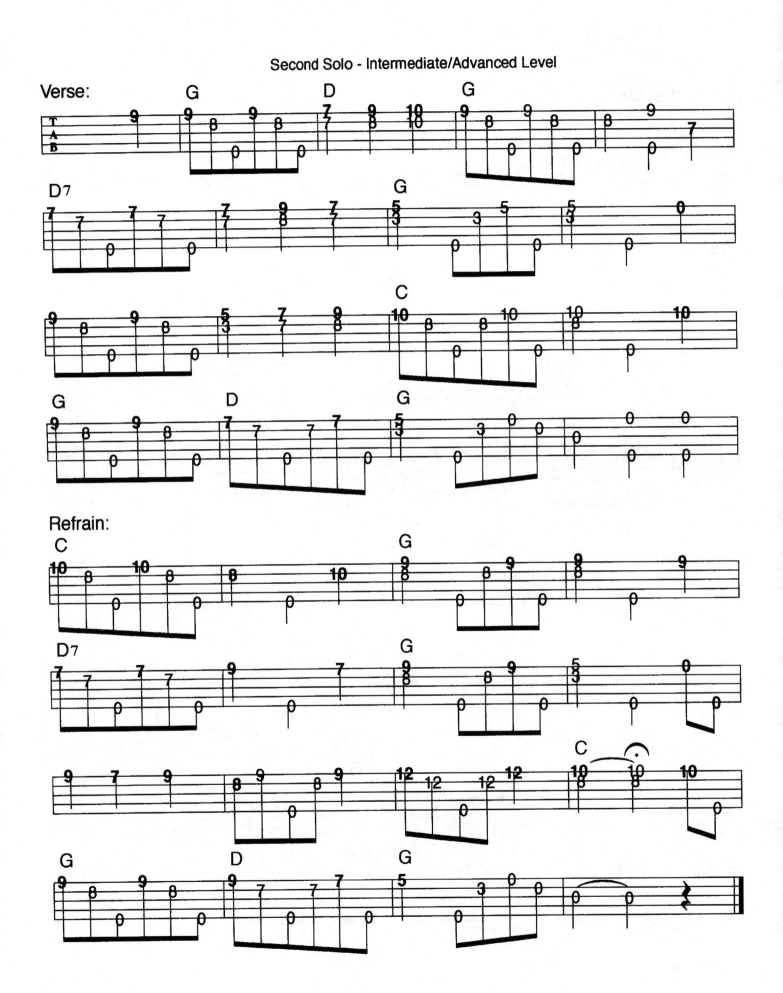

Drifting Too Far From The Shore

1) Out on the perilous deep,
Where dangers silently creep;
And storms so violently sweep,
You are drifting too far from the shore.

Refrain: Drifting too far from the shore*(from the shore)*
You are drifting too far from the shore*(peaceful shore)*
Come to Jesus today, let Him show you the way;
You are drifting too far from the shore.

2) Today, the tempest rolls high,
And the clouds overshadow the sky;
Sure death is hovering high;
You are drifting too far from the shore.

Refrain

3) Why meet a terrible fate,
Mercies abundantly wait,
Turn back before it's too late;
You are drifting too far from the shore.

Refrain

G Tuning:
DBGDg

Farther Along

Ability Level:
Beginner

J.R. Baxter, Jr.

W.B. Stevens

Second Solo - Intermediate Level

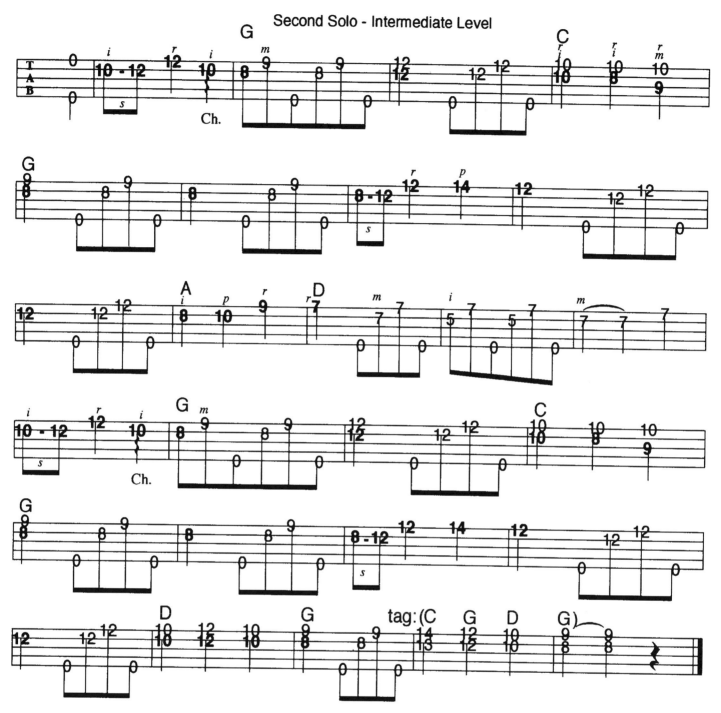

Refrain:
Farther along we'll know all about it; farther along we'll understand why.
Cheer up my brothers, live in the sunshine, We'll understand it all by and by.

2) When death has come and taken our loved ones, it leaves our home so lonely and dear,
Then do we wonder why others prosper; living so wicked year after year.

Refrain

3) When we see Jesus coming in glory; when he comes from his home in the sky.
Then we shall meet him in that bright mansion; we'll understand it, all by and by.

Refrain

The Great Speckled Bird

Traditional

The Great Speckled Bird

1) What a beautiful thought I am thinking
Concerning the Great Speckled Bird;
Remember her name is recorded
On the pages of pure shining gold.
All the other birds flocking 'round her
And she is despised by the squad;
But the Great Speckled Bird in the Bible
Is one with the great church of God.

2) All the other churches are against her;
They envy her glory and fame;
They hate her because she is chosen;
And has not denied Jesus' name.
Desiring to lower her standard;
They watch ev'ry move that she makes
They try to find fault with her teachings;
But they cannot find any mistakes.

3) She is spreading her wings for a journey;
She is going to leave by and by,
When the trumpet shall sound in the morning;
She will rise and go up in the sky.
In the presence of all her despisers;
With a song never uttered before,
She will rise and be gone in a moment;
Till the great tribulation is o'er.

4) I am glad to have learned of her meekness;
I am glad that my name's on the Book,
And I want to be one never fearing;
On the face of my Savior to look.
When He cometh descending from Heaven;
On the cloud, as He wrote in the Word,
I'll be joyfully carried up to meet Him;
On the wings of the Great Speckled Bird.

G Tuning:
DBGDg

He Leadeth Me!

Joseph H. Gilmore

Ability Level:
Intermediate

William B. Bradley

2) Sometimes 'mid scenes of deepest gloom,
Sometimes where Eden's bowers bloom;
By waters calm, o'er troubled sea,
Still, 'tis His hand that leadeth me.

Refrain

3) Lord, I would clasp Thy hand in mine,
Nor ever murmer nor repine;
Content, whatever lot I see,
Since 'tis my God that leadeth me.

Refrain

4) And when my task on earth is done,
When, by Thy grace, the victory's won;
E'en death's cold wave I will not flee,
Since God through Jordan leadeth me.

Refrain

Holy, Holy, Holy!

Reginald Heiber

John B. Dykes

Second Solo - Intermediate Level

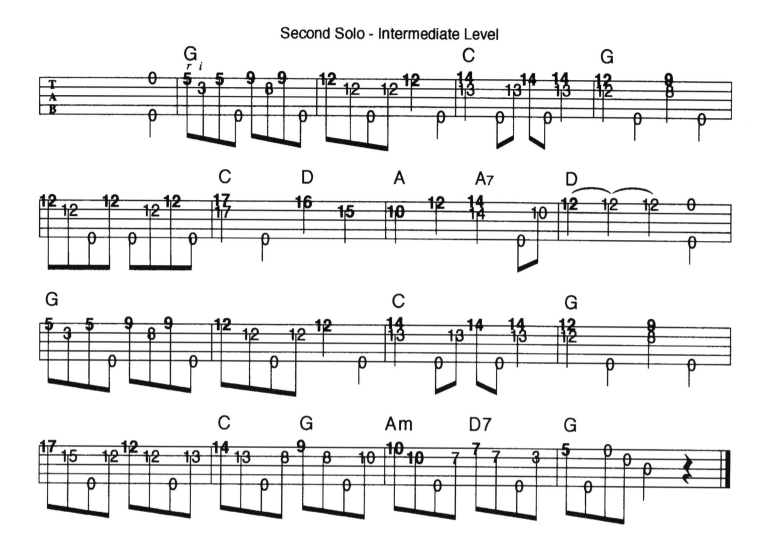

2) Holy, holy, holy! All the saints adore Thee,
Casting down their golden crowns around the glassy sea;
Cherubim and seraphim falling down before Thee,
Who wert, and art, and evermore shalt be.

3) Holy, holy, holy! Tho' the darkness hide Thee,
Tho' the eye of sinful man Thy glory may not see;
Only Thou art holy; there is none beside Thee,
Perfect in pow'r, in love and purity.

4) Holy, holy, holy! Lord God Almighty!
All Thy works shall praise Thy name, in earth and sky and sea;
Holy, holy, holy! Merciful and mighty!
God in three Persons, blessed Trinity!

I Am A Pilgrim

Traditional

I am a pil - grim and a strang - er trav'-lin'

through this wear-i-some land. But I've got a

home in that yon - der ci - ty good Lord, and it's

bass: oh, no it's not
not, not made by hand.

Second Solo - Intermediate Level

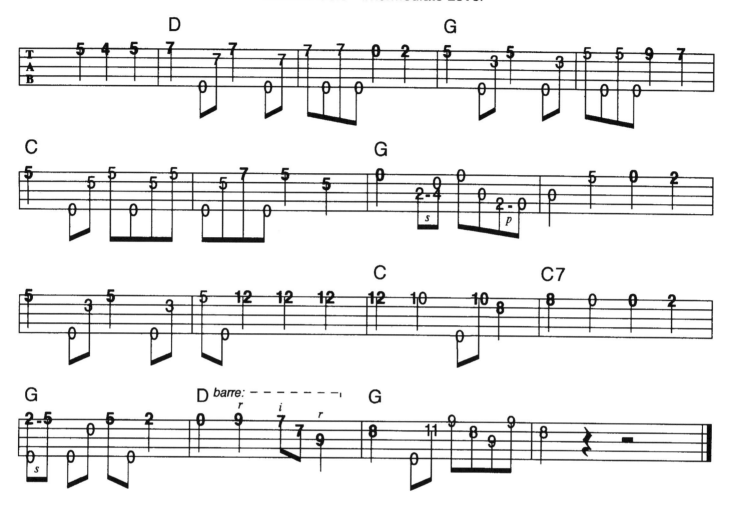

2) I got a mother, a sister and a brother
Who have gone this way before
I'm determined to go and see them, Good Lord
Over on that distant shore.

3) I'm going down to that river Jordan
Just to bathe my weary soul.
If I could touch but the hem of his garment, Good Lord
Well, I know it would make me whole.

G Tuning:
DBGDg

Ability Level:
Beginner/Intermediate

In The Garden

C. Austin Miles   C. Austin Miles

Refrain:

walks with me, And he talks with me, And he tells me I am his own; And the joy we share as we tar - ry there, None oth- er has e - ver known.

43

Second Solo: Intermediate Level

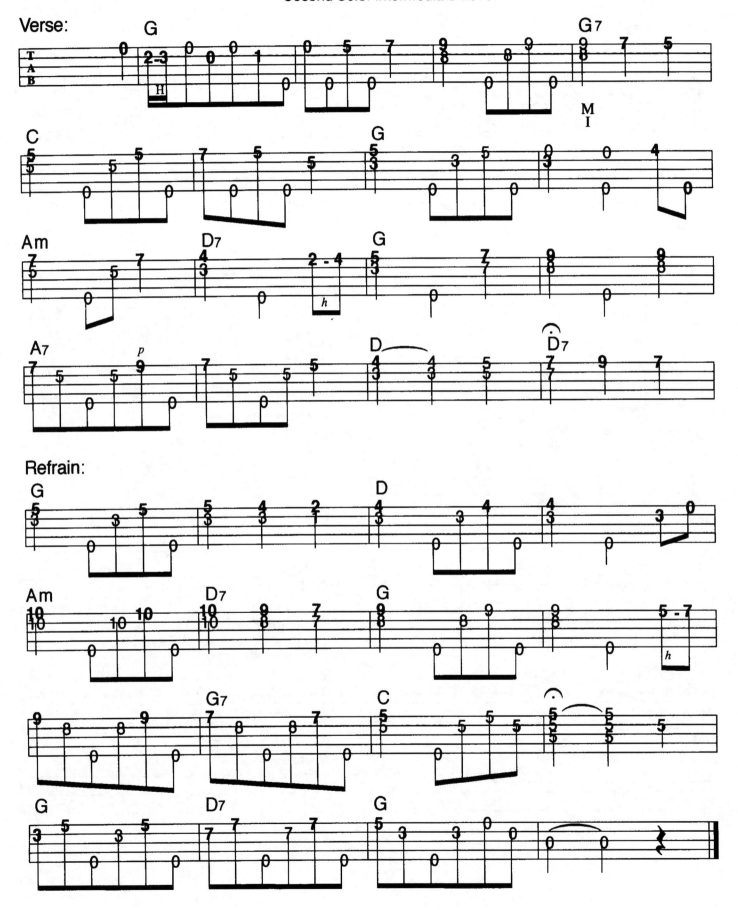

In The Garden

1) I come to the garden alone,
While the dew is still on the roses;
And the voice I hear, falling on my ear,
The Son of God discloses.

Refrain:
And he walks with me,
And he talks with me,
And he tells me I am his own;
And the joy we share as we tarry there,
None other has ever known.

2) He speaks, and the sound of his voice;
Is so sweet the birds hush their singing,
And the melody that He gave to me;
Within my heart is ringing.

Refrain

3) I'd stay in the garden with Him;
Though the night around me be falling
But he bids me go; Through the voice of woe,
His voice to me is calling.

Refrain

In The Sweet By And By

J.P. Webster

J.P. Webster

Refrain:

47

Second Solo - Intermediate/Advanced Level

48

In the Sweet By and By

1) There's a land that is fairer than day,
And by faith we can see it afar;
For the Father waits over the way
To prepare us a dwelling place there.

Refrain:
In the sweet (in the sweet)
By and by (by and by)
We shall meet on that beautiful shore;
In the sweet (in the sweet)
By and by (by and by)
We shall meet on that beautiful shore.

2) We shall sing on that beautiful shore;
The melodious songs of the blest,
And our spirits shall sorrow no more;
Not a sigh for the blessing of rest.

Refrain

3) To our bountiful Father above;
We will offer our tributes of praise;
For the glorious gift of his love;
And the blessings that hallow our days.

Refrain

G Tuning:
DBGDg

Ability Level:
Intermediate

Just A Closer Walk With Thee

Oscar Clute

Robert Jackson

I am weak but thou art strong.

Je - sus keep me from all wrong;

I'll be sat - is - fied as long as I

walk, let me walk close to Thee.

Refrain:

51

Verse/Refrain:

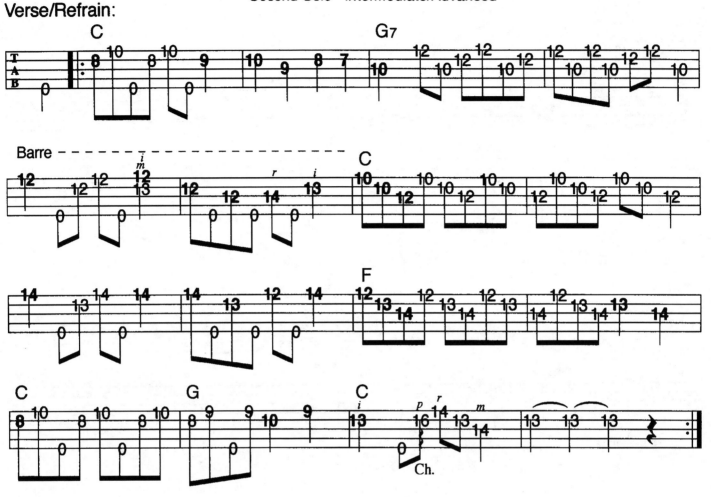

Just A Closer Walk With Thee

1) Through the days of toil that's near,
If I fall, dear Lord, who cares;
Who with me my burden shares?
Only Thee, dear Lord, only Thee.

Refrain:
Just a closer walk with Thee,
Grant it Jesus if you please;
Daily walking close to Thee,
Let it be, dear Lord, let it be.

2) When my troubled life is o'er,
Time for me will be no more;
Then guide me gently, safely home,
To Thy shore, dear Lord, to Thy shore.

Refrain

3) When life's sun sets in the west,
Lord, may I have done my best;
May I find sweet peace and rest,
In that home, happy home, of the blest.

Refrain

Just Over In The Glory Land

James W. Acuff

Emmett S. Dean

Refrain:

55

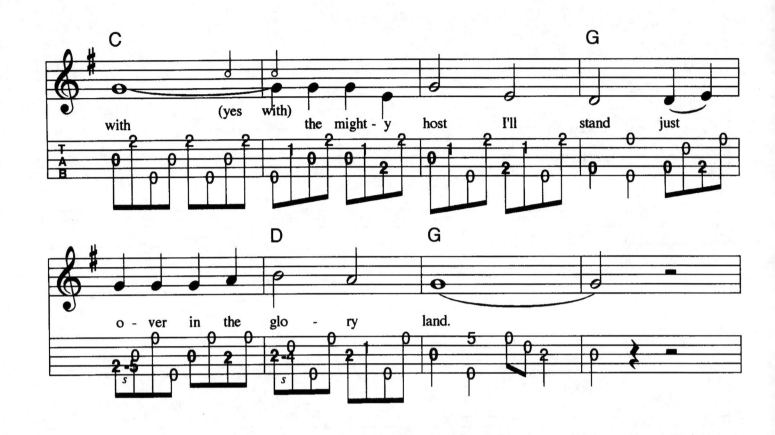

Just Over In The Glory Land

1) I've a home prepared where the saints abide,
Just over in the glory land;
And I long to be by my Savior's side,
Just over in the glory land.

Refrain: Just over (over, over) In the glory land,
I'll join (I'll join) the happy angel band;
Just over in the glory land.
Just over (over, over) in the glory land,
There with (yes, with) the mighty Host I'll stand;
Just over in the glory land.

2) I am on my way to those mansions fair,
Just over in the glory land;
There to sing God's praise and his glory share,
Just over in the glory land.

Refrain

3) What a joyful thought that my Lord I'll see,
Just over in the glory land;
And with kindred saved there forever be,
Just over in the glory land.

Refrain

4) With the bloodwashed throng I will shout and sing,
Just over in the glory land;
Glad hosannas to Christ, the Lord and King,
Just over in the glory land.

Refrain

G Tuning:
DBGDg

Ability Level:
Beginner/Intermediate

Keep On The Sunny Side Of Life

Ada Blenkhorn

J. Howard Entwisle

Refrain:

Keep on the sun- ny side Al - ways on the sun- ny side,

Keep on the sun- ny side of life, It will

help us ev - 'ry day it will bright - en all the way, If we

Keep on the sun - ny side of life.

Second Solo - Intermediate/Advanced Level

Keep On The Sunny Side Of Life

1) There's a dark and a troubled side of life,
There's a bright and sunny side, too.
Though we meet with the darkness and strife,
The sunny side we also may view.

Refrain:
Keep on the sunny side, Always on the sunny side;
Keep on the sunny side of life.
It will help us every day, it will brighten all the way,
If we keep on the sunny side of life.

2) Though the storm in its fury break today,
Crushing hopes that we cherished so dear;
Storm and cloud will in time pass way,
The sun again will shine bright and clear.

Refrain

3) Let us greet with song of hope each day,
Though the moments be cloudy or fair;
Let us trust in our Savior always,
Who keepeth every one in His care.

Refrain

Life's Railway To Heaven

M.E. Abbey

Charles D. Tillman

Refrain:

Sav - ior, thou wilt guide us 'til we reach that bliss - ful shore; where the an - gels wait to join us in God's grace for - ev - er more

Life's Railway To Heaven

1) Life is like a mountain railroad,
With an engineer that's brave.
We must make this run successful,
From the cradle to the grave.
Watch the hills, the curves and tunnels,
Never falter, never fail.
Keep your hand upon the throttle,
And your eye upon the rail.

Refrain: Blessed Savior, thou wilt guide us,
'Till we reach that blissful shore!
Where the angels wait to join us,
In God's grace forever more.

2) As you roll across the trestle,
Spanning Jordan's swelling tide
You behold the union depot,
Into which your train will glide.
There you'll meet the superintendent;
God the Father, God the Son
With a hearty, joyous greeting;
Weary pilgrim, welcome home!

Refrain

G Tuning:
DBGDg

Ability Level:
Beginner/Intermediate

The Lily Of The Valley

Charles W. Fry

William S. Hayes

I have found a friend in Je-sus He's ev-'ry-thing to me. He's the

fair-est of ten thou-sand to my soul; The

Li-ly of the Val-ley, in Him a-lone I see, All I

need to cleanse and make me ful-ly whole. In

66

Refrain:

Verse:

Refrain:

The Lily of the Valley

1) I have found a friend in Jesus, He's everything to me;
He's the fairest of ten thousand to my soul;
The Lily of the Valley, in Him alone I see,
All I need to cleanse and make me fully whole.

Refrain: In sorrow he's my comfort, in trouble he's my stay;
He tells me every care on him to roll.
He's the Lily of the Valley, the bright and morning star,
He's the fairest of ten thousand to my soul.

2) He all my grief has taken, and all my sorrows borne;
In temptation He's my strong and mighty tow'r;
I have all for him forsaken, and all my idols torn from my heart,
And now He keeps me by his pow'r.

Refrain: Tho' all the world forsake me, and Satan tempts me sore,
Thru Jesus I shall safely reach the goal;
He's the Lily of the Valley, the bright and morning star,
He's the fairest of ten thousand to my soul.

3) He will never, never leave me, nor yet forsake me here,
While I live by faith and do His blessed will;
A wall of fire about me, I've nothing now to fear;
With His manner He my hungry soul shall fill.

Refrain: Then sweeping up to glory, to see His blessed face,
Where rivers of delight shall ever roll;
He's the Lily of the Valley, the bright and morning star,
He's the fairest of ten thousand to my soul.

The Old Gospel Ship

Traditional

Refrain:

Second Solo - Intermediate/Advanced Level

Verse:

Refrain:

The Old Gospel Ship

1) I have good news to bring, and that is why I sing.
All my joys with you I'll share;
I'm going to take a trip in that old gospel ship
And go sailing through the air.

Refrain:
Oh, I'm gonna take a trip on that old gospel ship,
I'm going far beyond the sky;
Oh, I'm gonna shout and sing,
Until the heavens ring,
When I'm bidding this world goodbye.

2) Oh, I can scarcely wait, I know I'll not be late;
For I'll spend my time in prayer.
And when my ship comes in, I will leave this world of sin;
And go sailing through the air.

Refrain

3) If you're ashamed of me, you have no cause to be,
For with Christ I am an heir.
If too much fault you find, you will sure be left behind,
While I go sailing through the air.

Refrain

G Tuning:
DBGDg

( ) = passing chords, not
played by rhythm
instruments

Ability Level:
Beginner/Intermediate

The Old Rugged Cross

Rev. George Bennard

Rev. George Bennard

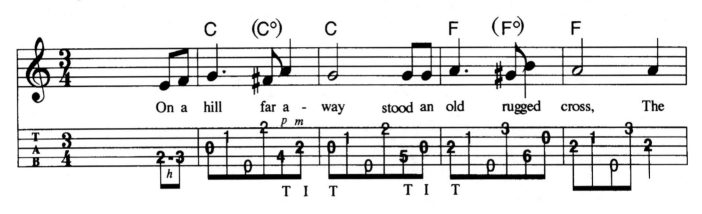

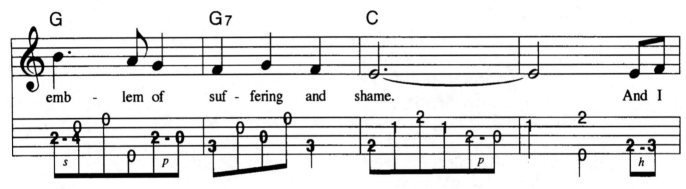

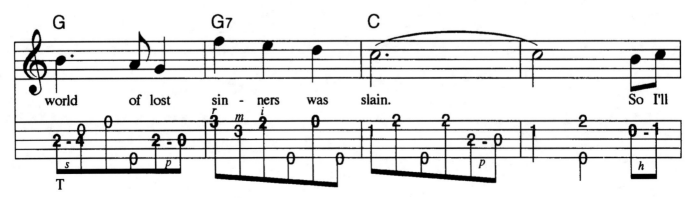

Refrain:

75

Second Solo - Intermediate/Advanced Level

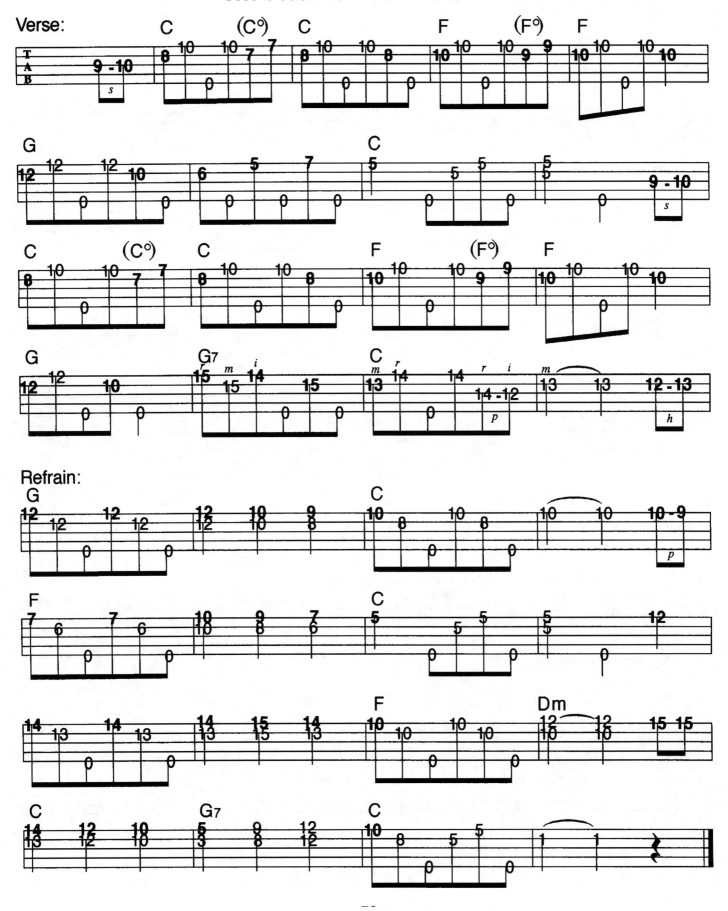

The Old Rugged Cross

1) On a hill far away stood an old rugged cross,
The emblem of suffering and shame.
And I love that old cross where the dearest and best
For a world of lost sinners was slain.

Refrain: So I'll cherish the old rugged cross,
'Til my trophies at last I lay down;
I will cling to the old rugged cross,
And exchange it some day for a crown.

2) Oh that old rugged cross, so despised by the world,
Has a wondrous attraction for me;
For the dear lamb of God left his glory above;
To bear it to dark calvary.

Refrain

3) In the old rugged cross, stained with blood so divine,
A wondrous beauty I see;
For 'twas on that old cross Jesus suffered and died;
To pardon and sanctify me.

Refrain

4) To the old rugged cross I will ever be true,
It's shame and reproach gladly bear;
Then He'll call me some day to my home far away;
Where his glory forever I'll share.

Refrain

G Tuning:
DBGDg

Old-Time Religion

Traditional

Give me that old time re - li - gion, give me that old time re-

li - gion, give me that old time re - li - gion, it's good e- nough for me.

Second Solo - Intermediate Level

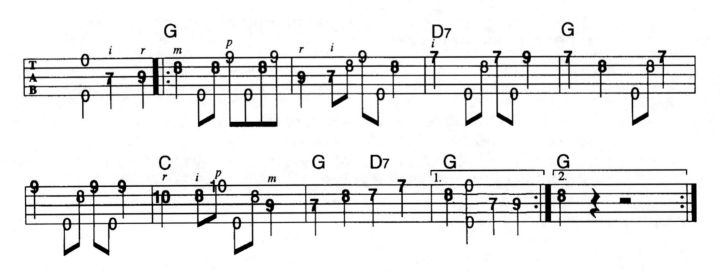

Old-Time Religion

1) Give me that old-time religion,
Give me that old-time religion,
Give me that old-time religion,
It's good enough for me.

2) It was good for Paul and Silas,
It was good for Paul and Silas,
It was good for Paul and Silas,
It's good enough for me.

3) It was good for our mothers,
It was good for our mothers,
It was good for our mothers,
It's good enough for me.

4) Makes me love everybody,
Makes me love everybody,
Makes me love everybody,
It's good enough for me.

5) It was precious to our fathers,
It was precious to our fathers,
It was precious to our fathers,
It's good enough for me.

6) It will take us all to heaven,
It will take us all to heaven,
It will take us all to heaven,
It's good enough for me.

G Tuning:
DBGDg

Precious Memories

J.B.F. Wright

J.B.F. Wright

Pre - cious mem'ries   un -   seen an- gels

sent   from some where to   my soul.

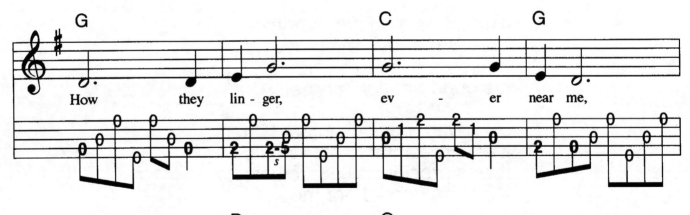

How   they   lin - ger,   ev -   er   near me,

And   the sa - cred past un - fold.

Refrain:

Second Solo - Intermediate/Advanced Level

Verse:

Refrain:

Precious Memories

1) Precious mem'ries, unseen angels,
Sent from somewhere to my soul;
How they linger, ever near me,
And the sacred past unfold.

Refrain:
Precious mem'ries, how they linger,
How they ever flood my soul!
In the stillness of the midnight,
Precious, sacred scenes unfold.

2) Precious father, loving mother,
Fly across the lonely years;
And old home scenes of my childhood,
In fond memory appear.

Refrain

3) In the stillness of the midnight,
Echoes from the past I hear;
Old time singing, gladness bringing;
From that lovely land somewhere.

Refrain

4) As I travel on life's pathway,
Know not what the years may hold;
As I ponder, hope grows fonder,
Precious mem'ries flood my soul.

Refrain

G Tuning:
DBGDg

Ability Level:
Beginner/Intermediate

Rock Of Ages

Agustus M. Toplady

Thomas Hastings

Rock of   a - ges cleft for me.   Let me hide   my-self in Thee.   Let the

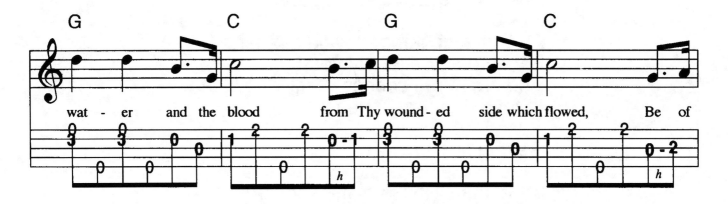

wat - er   and the blood   from Thy wound - ed   side which flowed,   Be of

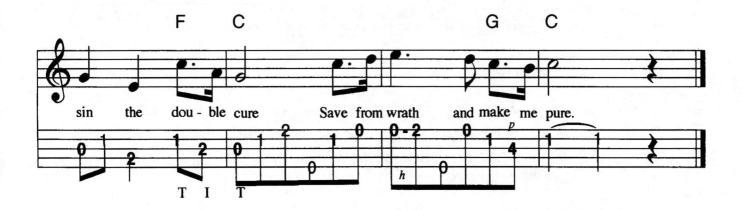

sin   the   dou - ble cure   Save from wrath   and make me pure.

84

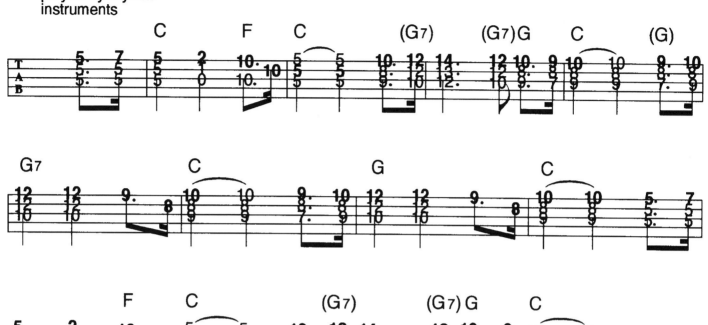

2) Not the labors of my hands, can fulfill Thy law's demands;
Could my zeal no respite know, could my tears forever flow,
All for sin could not atone, thou must save, and thou alone.

3) Nothing in my hand I bring, simply to Thy cross I cling;
Naked, come to Thee for dress, helpless look to Thee for grace;
Foul, I to the fountain fly; wash me, Savior, or I die.

4) While I draw this fleeting breath, when my eyelids close in death,
When I soar to worlds unknown, see Thee on Thy judgement throne,
Rock of Ages, cleft for me, let me hide myself in Thee.

Shall We Gather At The River

Robert Lowery

Robert Lowery

2) On the margin of the river,
Washing up it's silver spray,
We will walk and worship ever,
All the happy golden day.

Refrain

3) There we reach the shining river,
There we lay our burdens down.
Grace our spirits will deliver,
And provide a robe and crown.

Refrain

4) Soon we'll reach the shining river,
Soon our pilgrimage will cease.
Soon our happy hearts will quiver,
With the melody of peace.

Refrain

C Tuning:
DBGCg

Sweet Hour Of Prayer

William B. Bradbury

William B. Bradbury

Second Solo - Intermediate/Advanced Level

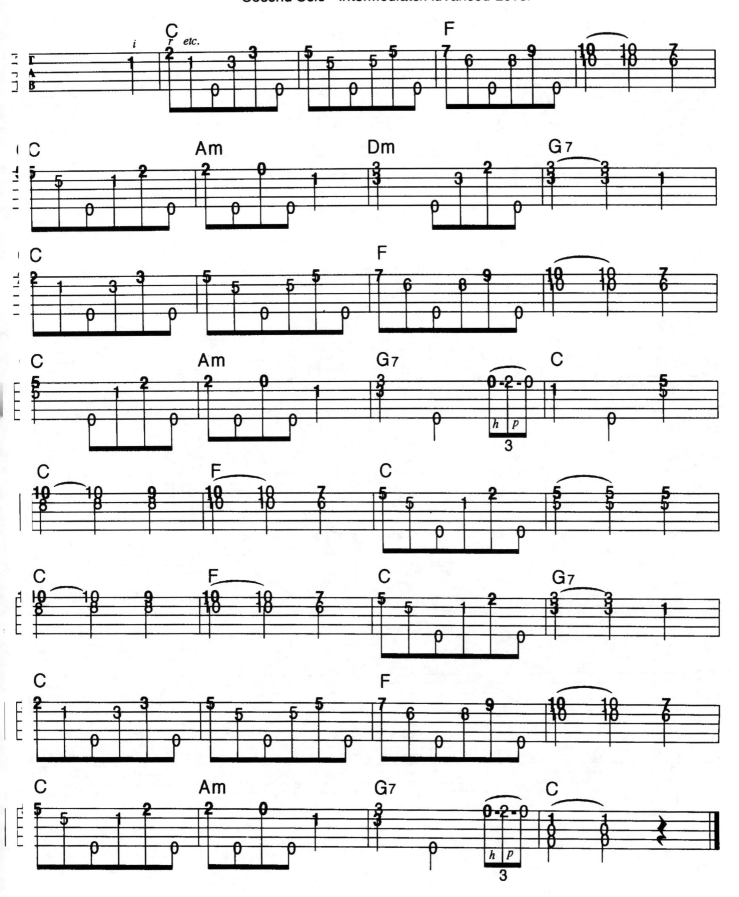

Sweet Hour of Prayer

1) Sweet hour of prayer! Sweet hour of prayer!
That calls me from a world of care,
And bids me at my father's throne,
Make all my wants and wishes known.
In seasons of distress and grief,
My soul has often found relief,
And oft escaped the temptor's snare;
By thy return, sweet hour of prayer!

2) Sweet hour of prayer! Sweet hour of prayer!
Thy wings shall my petition bear,
To Him whose truth and faithfulness,
Engage the waiting soul to bless;
And since he bids me seek His face,
Believe His Word and trust His Grace.
I'll trust on Him my every care,
And wait for thee, sweet hour of prayer.

3) Sweet hour of prayer! Sweet hour of prayer!
May I thy consolation share,
Till, from Mount Pisgah's lofty height,
I view my home, and take my flight;
This robe of flesh I'll drop and rise,
To seize the everlasting prize;
And shout while passing through the air,
Farewell, farewell, sweet hour of prayer.

G Tuning:
DBGDg

Ability Level:
Beginner/Intermediate

The Unclouded Day

Rev. J.K. Alwood

Rev. J.K. Alwood

Refrain:

Second Solo - Intermediate/Advanced Level

Verse:

Refrain:

The Unclouded Day

1) Oh, they tell me of a home far beyond the skies,
Oh, they tell me of a home far away;
Oh, they tell me of a home where no storm clouds rise;
Oh, they tell me of an unclouded day.

Refrain:
Oh, the land of cloudless day,
Oh, the land of an unclouded day.
Oh, they tell me of a home where no storm clouds rise;
Oh, they tell me of an unclouded day.

2) Oh, they tell me of a home where my friends have gone,
Oh they tell me of that land far away;
Where the tree of life is in eternal bloom,
Sheds it's fragrance thro' the unclouded day.

Refrain

3) Oh, they tell of a King in His beauty there,
And they tell me that mine eyes shall behold;
Where He sits on the throne that is whiter than snow,
In the city that is made of gold.

Refrain

4) Oh, they tell me that He smiles on His children there,
And His smile drives their sorrows all away;
And they tell me that no tears ever come again,
In that lovely land of unclouded day.

Refrain

What A Friend We Have In Jesus

Charles C. Converse

Charles C. Converse

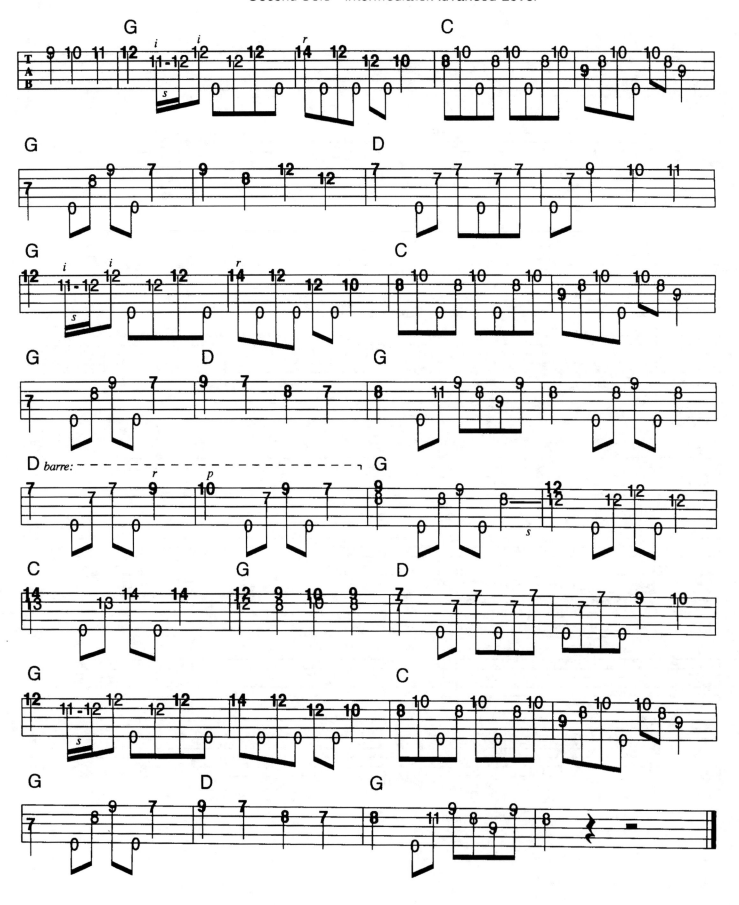

What A Friend We Have In Jesus

1) What a friend we have in Jesus,
All our sins and griefs to bear!
What a privilege to carry,
Everything to God in prayer!
Oh, what peace we often forfeit;
Oh, what needless pain we bear!
All because we do not carry
Everything to God in prayer.

2) Have we trials and temptations?
Is there trouble everywhere?
We should never be discouraged;
Take it to the Lord in prayer.
Can we find a friend so faithful,
Who will all our sorrows share?
Jesus knows our every weakness,
Take it to the Lord in prayer.

3) Are we weak and heavy laden,
Cumbered with a load of care?
Precious Savior, still our refuge,
Take it to the Lord in prayer.
Do thy friends despise, forsake thee?
Take it to the Lord in prayer;
In His arms He'll take and shield thee,
Thy wilt find a solace there.

Ability Level:
Beginner/Intermediate

When The Roll Is Called Up Yonder

James M. Black

James M. Black